P9-EDG-188

Table of Contents

Mark It!

1. b e d b u g
2. h e c t i c
3. u n p a c k
4. c l a s s i c
5. c a b i n
6. i n s p e c t
7. n a p k i n
8. s u b t r a c t
9. t e n n i s
10. n u t m e g
11. t r o p i c
12. v a n i s h

Read It!

1	hectic	nutmeg	inspect
2	napkin	tropic	subtract
3	tennis	bedbug	cabin
4	classic	unpack	vanish
5	inspect	tennis	bedbug
6	nutmeg	vanish	napkin
7	hectic	cabin	subtract

Challenging ⭐

	How many syllables?	🍎	📦	🖐️	🐙	☝️
1 robin	1　2					
2 flip	1　2					
3 grump	1　2					
4 bench	1　2					

More Challenging ⭐⭐

	How many syllables?	🍎	📦	🖐️	🐙	☝️
1 splash	1　2					
2 whiplash	1　2					
3 mantis	1　2					
4 fabric	1　2					

Most Challenging ⭐⭐⭐

	How many syllables?	🍎	📦	🖐️	🐙	☝️
1 crosshatch	1　2					
2 squint	1　2					
3 branch	1　2					
4 bankrupt	1　2					

Challenging ☆

1. insist on trips to Dublin

2. can finish dusting the shelf

3. cannot catch the rabbit for her

4. nutmeg and pumpkin at the picnic

More Challenging ☆☆

5. slip on the bathmat next to the bathtub

6. never with the British bobsled medic

7. would infect the bobcat with toxic runoff

8. to ask them about the windswept fishpond

Most Challenging ☆☆☆

9. hiccup when the suspect came jumping out

10. can carry a small satin sundress in her handbag

11. like to ride on the tram to see the classic quintet

12. make and crunch on the splendid relish sandwich

Challenging ☆

1. The bobcat cannot catch the swift rabbit. (7)

2. Give credit to Patrick for his transcript. (7)

3. We want them to expand the radish planting. (8)

4. Will you take nutmeg and pumpkin to the picnic? (9)

More Challenging ☆ ☆

5. You could slip on the bathmat next to the bathtub. (10)

6. Calvin must submit his test, so do not distract him. (10)

7. Jan can carry a small satin dress in her handbag. (10)

8. I expect you to finish that contract when you get back. (11)

Most Challenging ★ ☆ ☆

9. Can you make a plastic laptop for the contest by the end of today? (14)

10. My dad and I want the nonstop traffic to vanish before sunset. (12)

11. After the ride on the tram, we went to see the classic quintet. (13)

12. If you would like to have a mustang, you must be a spendthrift. (13)

Challenging Words ☆

1st Syllable   2nd Syllable

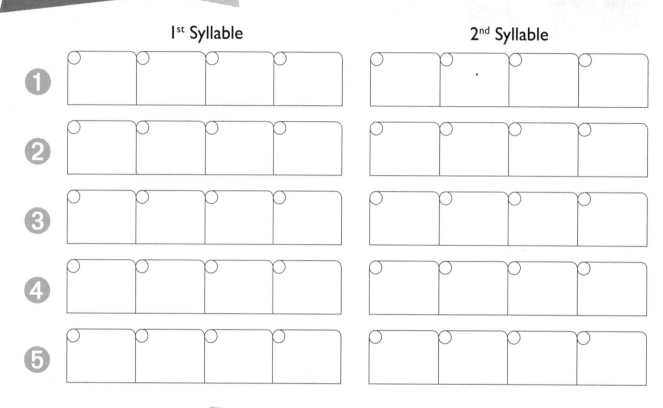

More Challenging Words ☆☆

1st Syllable   2nd Syllable

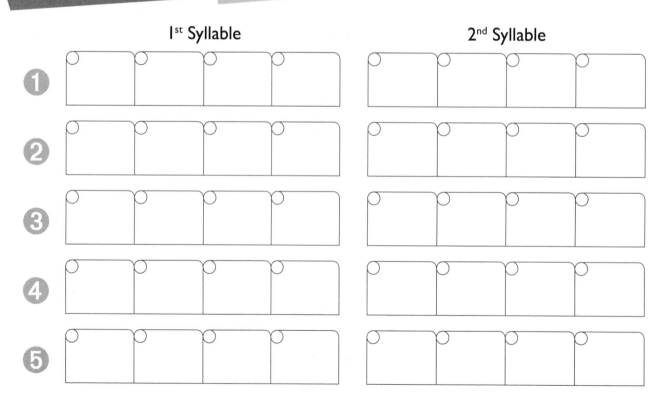

Mark It!

1. w e
2. d r y
3. s o
4. m y
5. s k y
6. b e

7. s h y
8. p r o
9. s h e
10. t r y
11. h e
12. w h y

Read It!

1. we   why   dry
2. so   my   be
3. shy   pro   she
4. sky   try   he
5. be   pro   dry
6. why   she   sky
7. my   so   try

Challenging ⭐

	Syllable		Vowel Sound	
	Open	Closed	Long	Short
1 pro	✓		✓	
2 rug		✓		✓
3 fly	✓		✓	
4 must		✓		✓

More Challenging ⭐⭐

	Syllable		Vowel Sound	
	Open	Closed	Long	Short
1 best		✓		✓
2 shy	✓		✓	
3 we				
4 glad		✓		✓

Most Challenging ⭐⭐⭐

	Syllable		Vowel Sound	
	Open	Closed	Long	Short
1 she	✓		✓	
2 shred		✓		✓
3 plant		✓		✓
4 try	✓		✓	

Challenging ☆

1 will credit him and me

2 so she will not go

3 will we all look into

4 has eggnog that is so good

More Challenging ★ ☆

5 no dry satin fabric left for him

6 to try the pumpkin sandwich

7 she began to look for a wombat

8 will ask him why the catfish swam

Most Challenging ★ ★ ☆

9 look at it vanish into the sky

10 until Willis is a pro locksmith

11 could look at my sluggish jog

12 so the brown rabbit can inspect the grass

Challenging ☆

1 She has whiplash from the big crash. (7)

2 Go to Dublin with him to finish the cabin. (9)

3 I will try to be the best mascot around. (9)

4 He put it into the fishpond with a splash. (9)

More Challenging ☆☆

5 You could try to get him a job as a milkman. (11)

6 Grant, the tennis pro, has to finish the match. (9)

7 My radish dish will be the hit of the potluck. (10)

8 We were upset by the tick tock of the clock. (10)

Most Challenging ★ ☆ ☆

9 Please look to the sky before you try to fly. (10)

10 Elvis ran right by me after he lost his pet chipmunk. (11)

11 When he ate the sandwich, he found a plastic tag in it. (12)

12 The man put out a trap, so the catfish swam into the fishnet. (13)

Challenging Words ⭐

1. | S | h | e | | | She

2. | Sh | e | d | | | Shed

3. | W | e | | | | We

4. | W | e | t | | | Wet

5. | Wh | y | | | | Why

More Challenging Words ⭐⭐

1. | P | r | o | | | Pro

2. | P | r | o | p | | Prop

3. | C | r | y | | | cry

4. | S | k | y | | | sky

5. | t | r | a | sh | | trash

Mark It!

1. m o t e l
2. h i k i n g
3. b a s i c
4. p r o g r a m
5. z e r o
6. d e p e n d

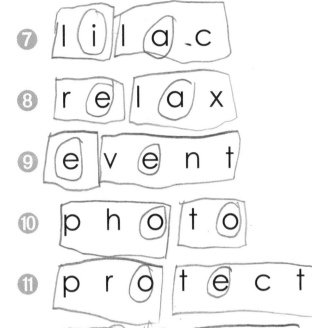

7. l i l a c
8. r e l a x
9. e v e n t
10. p h o t o
11. p r o t e c t
12. b e y o n d

Read It!

1	motel	lilac	relax
2	zero	depend	protect
3	basic	relax	photo
4	hiking	program	basic
5	depend	motel	event
6	beyond	hiking	lilac
7	zero	event	program

Word Sort

Challenging

	1st Syllable		2nd Syllable	
	Closed	Open	Closed	Open
① be•gan		✓	✓	
② den•tist	✓		✓	
③ pic•nic	✓		✓	
④ tri•pod		✓	✓	

More Challenging

	1st Syllable		2nd Syllable	
	Closed	Open	Closed	Open
① in•vent	✓		✓	
② Ve•nus		✓	✓	
③ ba•sic		✓	✓	
④ jum•bo	✓			✓

Most Challenging

	1st Syllable		2nd Syllable	
	Closed	Open	Closed	Open
① dish•pan	✓		✓	
② men•u	✓			✓
③ e•rupt				
④ bla•zing				

Phrases to Read

Challenging ☆

1. about the picnic menu

2. could run by the robot rabbit

3. uphill where the motel is

4. will take the banjo class

More Challenging ☆☆

5. could not go as fast as Iris

6. willing to defend and protect

7. where the green banjo could be

8. to take a jumbo helping at lunch

Most Challenging ☆☆☆

9. see six zigzags in the text

10. go rest and relax under the lilacs

11. will play any good music at the shindig

12. show respect in public by standing still

Sentences to Read

Challenging ☆

① Take a quick look over the long menu. (8)

② Iris could go by the robot rabbit in a rush. (10)

③ Where is the black pup sitting by the motel? (9)

④ Which program would you like to try, music or math? (10)

More Challenging ☆☆

⑤ It is too humid to go take a jog by the fishpond. (12)

⑥ Justin could not ride as fast as Ingrid, but he did try. (12)

⑦ Are you willing to defend and protect the chipmunk? (9)

⑧ Ben could see your classic green banjo at the event. (10)

Most Challenging ⭐ ⭐ ☆

⑨ I saw you take a jumbo helping of relish at the picnic. (12)

⑩ Where did Calvin begin to find six complex texts about catfish? (11)

⑪ Will the band play or sing any good music at the twin's shindig? (13)

⑫ My mom said I could show respect at the public expo by standing still. (14)

Challenging Words ⭐

1st Syllable   2nd Syllable

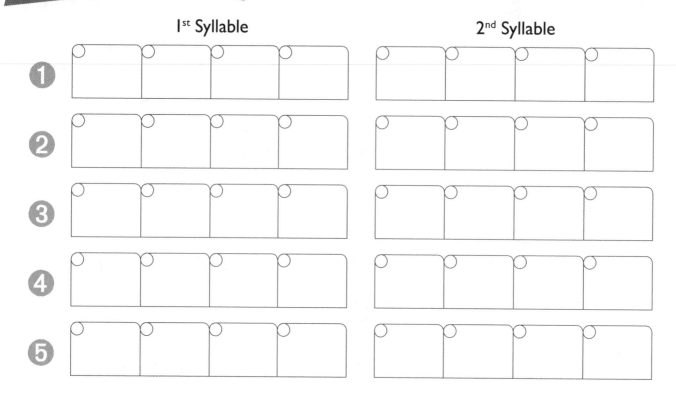

1
2
3
4
5

More Challenging Words ⭐⭐

1st Syllable   2nd Syllable

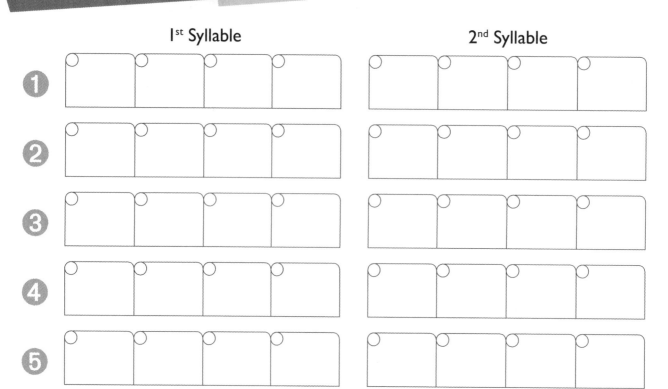

1
2
3
4
5

Detective Work ———————————

Mark It!

1. w a g o n
2. l a b e l
3. z e b r a
4. c o n f e s s
5. t o t a l
6. d r a g o n
7. c o m m a
8. o v a l
9. t r i p l e t
10. b o n u s
11. s a l a d
12. a d u l t

Read It!

1. adult	label	wagon
2. zebra	salad	dragon
3. oval	triplet	comma
4. confess	total	bonus
5. label	oval	zebra
6. salad	confess	adult
7. zebra	comma	triplet

 # Word Sort

 Challenging ☆

	1st Syllable		2nd Syllable		
	Closed	Open	Closed	Open	Schwa?
1 ba•con					
2 e•vent					
3 clos•et					
4 si•lent					

 More Challenging ☆ ☆

	1st Syllable		2nd Syllable		
	Closed	Open	Closed	Open	Schwa?
1 re•lax					
2 hic•cup					
3 jack•et					
4 a•dopt					

 **Most Challenging** ☆ ☆ ☆

	1st Syllable		2nd Syllable		
	Closed	Open	Closed	Open	Schwa?
1 he•ro					
2 chil•dren					
3 lock•smith					
4 mam•mal					

Challenging ☆

1. label on the old relish

2. is about to happen here

3. ate more than one dozen bagels

4. children and adults came here

More Challenging ☆☆

5. about the frozen lemon punch

6. model the classic satin dress

7. saw a gallon trashcan by the wall

8. will look over here for any lost items

Most Challenging ☆☆☆

9. around the old zebra and rabbit pen

10. will listen to any command you give

11. find the secret gift under the tall shelf

12. saw a yellow dragon in the frozen tundra

Challenging ☆

1. Did you look at the label on the old relish? (9)

2. Sunset is about to happen over the hilltop. (8)

3. Did you ask about the frozen lemon punch? (8)

4. Sam saw a gallon trashcan over by the wall. (9)

More Challenging ☆☆

5. Bella wants an oval pendant for her grad gift. (9)

6. The cactus I saw in the plastic pot was green. (10)

7. If you want your lost item back, look over here. (10)

8. Children and adults came here to pick a pumpkin. (9)

Most Challenging ⭐⭐☆

9 Did Jackson eat any of the dozen bagels today? (9)

10 My dog, Brenda, will listen to any command you give. (10)

11 Emma, will you try to find the secret gift under your tall shelf? (13)

12 Jason saw an old, yellow dragon here in the frozen tundra, and he ran! (14)

Spell It!

Challenging Words ☆

1st Syllable	2nd Syllable
①	o
②	e
③	e
④	u
⑤ a	

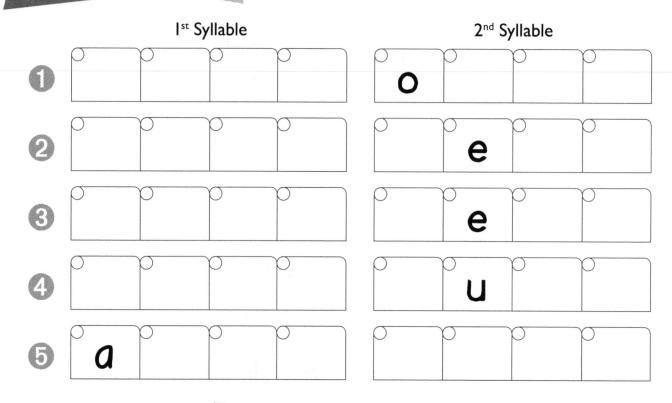

More Challenging Words ☆ ☆

1st Syllable	2nd Syllable
①	o
②	u
③	a
④	e
⑤	e

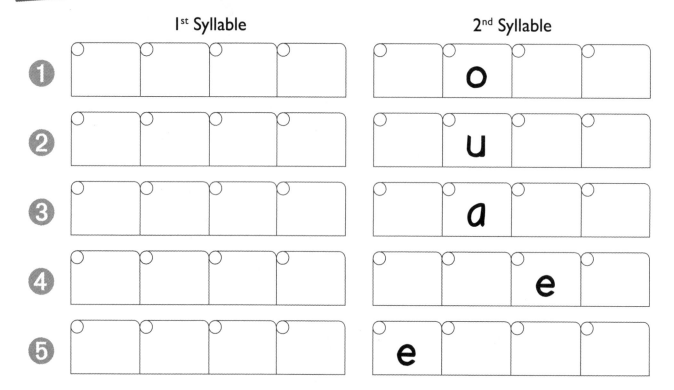

Mark It!

1. b a k e
2. c h a s e
3. b r o k e
4. c u t e
5. z o n e
6. f l a m e
7. a p e
8. c r i m e
9. g l o b e
10. t h e m e
11. g r a p e
12. p l a n e

Read It!

1. bake   broke   flame
2. globe   cute   chase
3. plane   theme   grape
4. crime   flame   zone
5. grape   chase   bake
6. theme   plane   ape
7. zone   broke   cute

Word Sort

Challenging

Syllable			Vowel Phoneme	
Closed	Open	VCE	Long	Short

❶ date

❷ we

❸ pal

❹ use

More Challenging ☆☆

Syllable			Vowel Phoneme	
Closed	Open	VCE	Long	Short

❶ shine

❷ quit

❸ trip

❹ be

Most Challenging ☆☆☆

Syllable			Vowel Phoneme	
Closed	Open	VCE	Long	Short

❶ scrape

❷ sly

❸ spin

❹ frame

Challenging ☆

1. over by the safe lake

2. must ask to use the rake

3. could take a very big bite

4. to skate on the little pond

More Challenging ☆ ☆

5. depend on a line to save a life

6. just broke her little blue locket

7. can ask around about the long, white cape

8. see the very wide plant by his gate

Most Challenging ☆ ☆ ☆

9. make me put on a long apron before I bake

10. will write a very long note to say thank you

11. problem with the scale made the rate go up

12. shine the yellow lamp over the broken game

Challenging ☆

1 Will you bake a lemon cake for the bride? (9)

2 Cut down the pine over by the lake to make space. (11)

3 You must ask to use the rake and the basket. (10)

4 Jackson will want to skate on the little local pond. (10)

More Challenging ☆ ☆

5 The oval lamp was broken after the long quake. (9)

6 Greta just broke her little blue locket in class. (9)

7 My rabbit could take a very big bite of the frozen cake. (12)

8 If the white cape is lost, you can ask around about it. (12)

Most Challenging ★★☆

9 Before I bake, my mom will make me put on a long apron. (13)

10 Emma, would you like to write a very long note to say thank you? (14)

11 I will help you fix the broken game if you shine the lamp over it. (15)

12 Down in the secret cave is a very warm home for the panda, hidden from the wind. (17)

Spell It!

Challenging Words ⭐

1.

2.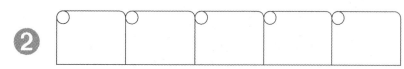

3.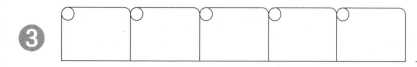

4.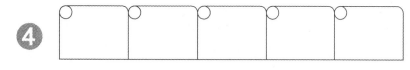

5.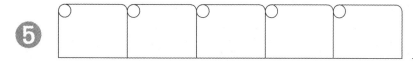

More Challenging Words ⭐⭐

1.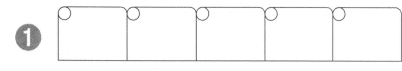

2.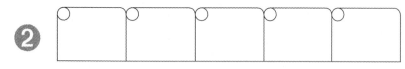

3.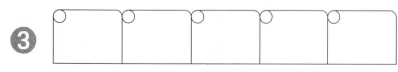

4.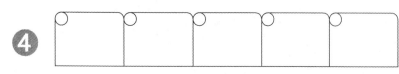

5.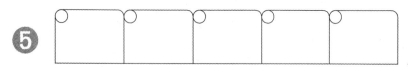

Mark It!

1. p a n c a k e
2. m i s t a k e
3. t r o m b o n e
4. h a n d m a d e
5. i n s i d e
6. t r a p e z e

7. c u p c a k e
8. e s c a p e
9. a t h l e t e
10. r e m o t e
11. l u n c h t i m e
12. e x p l o d e

Read It!

1. pancake   explode   cupcake
2. lunchtime   trombone   inside
3. trapeze   athlete   handmade
4. mistake   remote   escape
5. explode   trapeze   athlete
6. inside   lunchtime   pancake
7. escape   cupcake   mistake

 # Word Sort

Challenging ☆

	1st Syllable			2nd Syllable			
	Closed	Open	VCE	Closed	Open	VCE	Schwa?

① e•rase

② fish•bone

③ tad•pole

④ ig•nite

More Challenging ☆ ☆

	1st Syllable			2nd Syllable			
	Closed	Open	VCE	Closed	Open	VCE	Schwa?

① com•pete

② rock•slide

③ a•lone

④ bath•robe

Most Challenging ☆ ☆ ☆

	1st Syllable			2nd Syllable			
	Closed	Open	VCE	Closed	Open	VCE	Schwa?

① de•bate

② pave•ment

③ trans•late

④ frus•trate

Challenging ☆

1. erase the last name, too

2. a good pancake at lunchtime

3. know how to make it explode

4. around the campsite by the lake

More Challenging ☆ ☆

5. cannot know the secret handshake

6. know every kid on the event invite list

7. upgrade the command on my website

8. athlete likes to run a mile around the lake

Most Challenging ☆ ☆ ☆

9. know how to frustrate all of the irate cavemen

10. was too late to compete for the top athlete spot

11. cannot chase the white rabbit into the landslide

12. made a good, long cape for every hero costume

1 Be safe when you are home alone. (7)

2 Kate, will you erase the last name, too? (8)

3 If you explode with a yell, it will be a mistake. (11)

4 Did you write a note about the pancake at lunchtime? (10)

More Challenging ☆ ☆

5 Do you know how to upgrade the code on my website? (11)

6 Look for every good cupcake shop around the block. (9)

7 We set up five tents around the campsite by the lake. (11)

8 The brave caveman will frustrate his wife with his grunt. (10)

Most Challenging ☆ ☆ ☆

⑨ For Jake, it was a small milestone to drive around the block. (12)

⑩ If you do not know the secret handshake, I will not let you inside. (14)

⑪ I hope it is not too late to compete in the top athlete contest. (14)

⑫ It would be good if you could make a red cape for every costume. (14)

Challenging Words ☆

1st Syllable   2nd Syllable

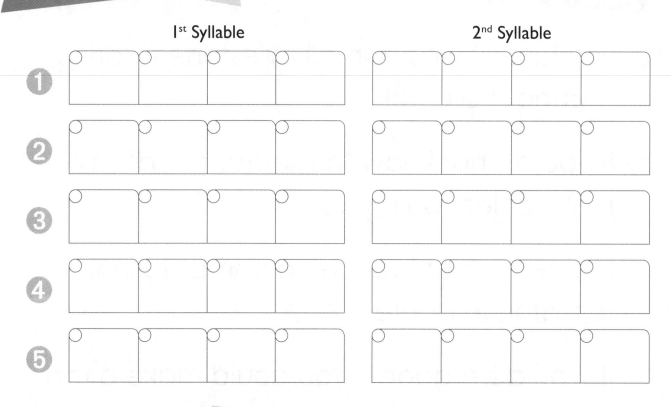

1
2
3
4
5

More Challenging Words ☆☆

1st Syllable   2nd Syllable

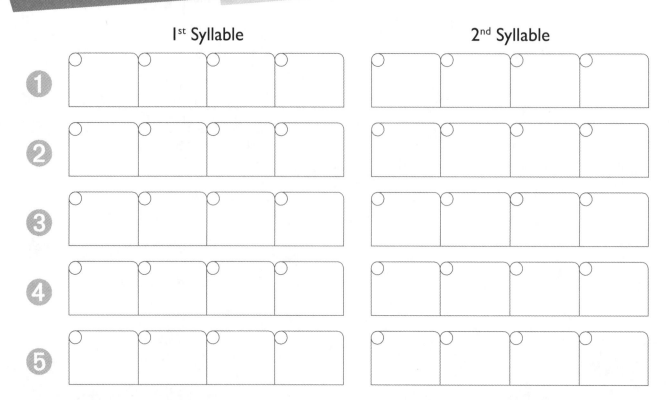

1
2
3
4
5

Mark It!

1. b e a d
2. s t a y
3. f e e d
4. g r a i n
5. t w e e t
6. p l a i n

7. b r a i d
8. s p e e d
9. t r a y
10. s q u e a k
11. s c r e e n
12. c h a i r

Read It!

1. bead   squeak   away
2. feed   speed   chain
3. tweet   grain   braid
4. braid   stay   plain
5. tray   feed   squeak
6. screen   bead   tweet
7. chain   tray   screen

Word Sort

Challenging ☆

	How many syllables?	1st Syllable			2nd Syllable		
		Closed	Open	Vowel Team	Closed	Open	Vowel Team
1 team	1 2						
2 delay	1 2						
3 sweep	1 2						
4 faith	1 2						

More Challenging ☆☆

	How many syllables?	1st Syllable			2nd Syllable		
		Closed	Open	Vowel Team	Closed	Open	Vowel Team
1 wheat	1 2						
2 between	1 2						
3 bleed	1 2						
4 asleep	1 2						

Most Challenging ☆☆☆

	How many syllables?	1st Syllable			2nd Syllable		
		Closed	Open	Vowel Team	Closed	Open	Vowel Team
1 afraid	1 2						
2 backseat	1 2						
3 scream	1 2						
4 upstream	1 2						

Challenging ☆

1 after the picnic next time

2 the bees and fleas fly away

3 will not swim away upstream

4 feed the grain to the pretty deer

More Challenging ☆☆

5 going to speed down the street

6 think about the messy pig's squeal

7 gave away a sweet cupcake

8 think she is going to replay the game

Most Challenging ☆☆☆

9 must study to maintain good grades

10 agreed on going after the late event

11 contains a pretty bead for the chain

12 after you clean the pancake from your plate

1 Jean cannot stand the pig's squeal. (6)

2 Think before you speed down the old street. (10)

3 If you attack, the bees and fleas will fly away. (10)

4 The chain will contain a pretty plastic bead. (8)

More Challenging ☆ ☆

5 We agreed on going home right after the late event. (10)

6 Did you prepay to see the screenplay, or was it free? (11)

7 Jay will not complain about feeding grain to the deer. (10)

8 Brady must study to maintain good grades and get a prize. (11)

9. After you clean the pancake from your sloppy plate, we will go. (12)

10. Steve gave some sweet candy away because he feels full. (10)

11. If you do not think about the pain, you will not be afraid. (13)

12. We all agree to get the green tree to put on our deck. (13)

Spell It!

Challenging Words ☆

1.

2.

3.

4.

5.

More Challenging Words ☆☆

1st Syllable	2nd Syllable
1.	
2.	
3.	
4.	
5.	

Detective Work

Mark It!

1. c o a t
2. f r i g h t
3. g r o a n
4. b r i g h t
5. c o a c h
6. t h r o a t
7. f l i g h t
8. f o a m
9. g o a l
10. r o a s t
11. m i g h t
12. t h i g h

Read It!

1. coat   foam   throat
2. flight   fright   goal
3. thigh   roast   coat
4. throat   might   groan
5. bright   flight   fright
6. coach   bright   might
7. roast   thigh   coach

Word Sort

Challenging ☆

	How many Syllables?	1st Syllable			2nd Syllable		
		Closed	Open	Vowel Team	Closed	Open	Vowel Team
1 light	1 2						
2 busload	1 2						
3 toast	1 2						
4 raincoat	1 2						

More Challenging ☆☆

	How many Syllables?	1st Syllable			2nd Syllable		
		Closed	Open	Vowel Team	Closed	Open	Vowel Team
1 coast	1 2						
2 cocoa	1 2						
3 shipload	1 2						
4 flashlight	1 2						

Most Challenging ☆☆☆

	How many Syllables?	1st Syllable			2nd Syllable		
		Closed	Open	Vowel Team	Closed	Open	Vowel Team
1 boast	1 2						
2 delight	1 2						
3 frightful	1 2						
4 upload	1 2						

Challenging ☆

1 at the sight of the lifeboat

2 before the quake last night

3 put on a raincoat for your walk

4 has been roaming down the oak path

More Challenging ☆☆

5 hall has been toasty before

6 walk to the whaleboat deck

7 take an oath before you go

8 before you make hot cocoa again

Most Challenging ☆☆☆

9 who has a slight scratch in her throat

10 upload the dragon program again

11 brightest to walk by the roadside at night

12 who asks for toast and oatmeal every day

 Challenging ☆

1. The dogs roam down the oak path again. (8)

2. At the sight of the lifeboat, I swam fast. (9)

3. Who fell asleep before the quake last night? (8)

4. Gail might have been on the sailboat before it left. (10)

More Challenging ☆ ☆

5. I do not like foamy black coffee with my toast. (10)

6. Who can make me some oatmeal and cocoa before class? (10)

7. Mom will make me put on a raincoat for my walk. (11)

8. The light inside has been too bright for the children taking the test. (13)

Most Challenging ★ ★ ☆

⑨ If I reach my goal, I can sleep in my light blue tent again. (14)

⑩ David had a slight scratch in his throat before he went to sleep. (13)

⑪ When you walk out on the whaleboat deck, you may slip. (11)

⑫ I found a white wallet by the roadside last night, but I gave it back. (15)

Spell It!

Challenging Words ☆

1 [ ] [ ] [ ] [ ] [ ]

2 [ ] [ ] [ ] [ ] [ ]

3 [ ] [ ] [ ] [ ] [ ]

4 [ ] [ ] [ ] [ ] [ ]

5 [ ] [ ] [ ] [ ] [ ]

More Challenging Words ☆ ☆

1st Syllable	2nd Syllable

1 [ ] [ ] [ ] [ ]   [ ] [ ] [ ] [ ]

2 [ ] [ ] [ ] [ ]   [ ] [ ] [ ] [ ]

3 [ ] [ ] [ ] [ ]   [ ] [ ] [ ] [ ]

4 [ ] [ ] [ ] [ ]   [ ] [ ] [ ] [ ]

5 [ ] [ ] [ ] [ ]   [ ] [ ] [ ] [ ]

Mark It!

1. l a s t e d
2. q u a c k e d
3. t i l t e d
4. l e a n e d
5. p l a n t e d
6. p r a y e d
7. s n i f f e d
8. s t i t c h e d
9. t w i s t e d
10. s o a k e d
11. g r o a n e d
12. s t r a n d e d

Read It!

1	groaned	tilted	sniffed
2	prayed	twisted	quacked
3	leaned	groaned	soaked
4	planted	lasted	tilted
5	quacked	stitched	twisted
6	lasted	stranded	leaned
7	soaked	sniffed	planted

 # Word Sort

 Challenging

	How many syllables?		Adds syllable /ed/	Adds sound /d/ or /t/
1 packed	1	2		
2 tested	1	2		
3 tweeted	1	2		
4 matched	1	2		

 More Challenging

	How many syllables?		Adds syllable /ed/	Adds sound /d/ or /t/
1 roasted	1	2		
2 blended	1	2		
3 fetched	1	2		
4 grasped	1	2		

 **Most Challenging**

	How many syllables?		Adds syllable /ed/	Adds sound /d/ or /t/
1 delayed	1	2		
2 scratched	1	2		
3 squinted	1	2		
4 stained	1	2		

Challenging ☆

1. cleaned all her own items

2. sad when his frosted cone melted

3. rocked and hummed to her own baby

4. checked the stalled bus in the street

More Challenging ☆☆

5. grunted because they were stranded

6. always squinted to see the small print

7. splashed around after the rain ended

8. rushed to help the lady because she screamed

Most Challenging ☆☆☆

9. sprinted away after he cracked his own lamp

10. always brushed the frizzed mane on the pony

11. panted because they dashed to catch the bus

12. goes to get the only thing he wished and hoped for

Challenging ☆

1. The lady was stranded on her own beach. (8)

2. Andy twisted the rope and docked the boat. (8)

3. Colleen rented a bike to ride down her own street. (10)

4. Steve goes to get the only thing he wished for. (10)

More Challenging ☆ ☆

5. Bobby stacked the pile of stuff, and Nicole lifted it. (10)

6. Dad fussed and yelled because Jane always blasted the music. (10)

7. The children only splashed and played when the rain stopped. (10)

8. Only the frosted glass with the chilled punch in it cracked. (11)

Most Challenging ★ ★ ★

9 Faith tended to her pony and always brushed his thick mane. (11)

10 Did your hand bleed when you pricked it on the rose plant? (12)

11 Maxwell checked out the rusted cab that had stalled on the road. (12)

12 David screamed when he twisted his leg as he sprinted down the beach. (13)

Challenging Words ⭐

1

2

3

4

5

More Challenging Words ⭐⭐

1ˢᵗ Syllable	2ⁿᵈ Syllable

1

2

3

4

5

Mark It!

1. t a l l e r
2. l i g h t i n g
3. f r o s t e d
4. t a x e s
5. d r e a m i n g
6. r e s t e d
7. c r u t c h e s
8. b r i g h t e r
9. l o a d i n g
10. h i g h e r
11. s t a c k i n g
12. c o a c h e s

Read It!

1	crutches	stacking	brighter
2	rested	brighter	loading
3	taxes	lighting	coaches
4	dreaming	taller	frosted
5	stacking	rested	higher
6	taller	frosted	taxes
7	higher	crutches	dreaming

Word Sort

Challenging ☆

	-er	-ed	-s	-es	-ing

1 faster

2 days

3 fizzes

4 dusted

More Challenging ☆☆

	-er	-ed	-s	-es	-ing

1 chilled

2 sweets

3 teacher

4 spending

Most Challenging ☆☆☆

	-er	-ed	-s	-es	-ing

1 slanted

2 raincoats

3 groaning

4 batches

Challenging ☆

1. write both of the lists

2. shines brighter than the sun

3. not faster to delay the plane

4. does not study for the tests

More Challenging ☆ ☆

5. clutching both of his crutches

6. faster than the speeding trains

7. want to be a runner and a singer

8. helper will give our teacher a rest

Most Challenging ☆ ☆ ☆

9. roams far from our rented home

10. eating cupcakes right before bedtime

11. will write but does not like reading novels

12. sketched the roses to give to his grandma

Challenging ☆

1. Does the lamp shine brighter than the sun? (8)

2. Will we get there faster if they delay our planes? (10)

3. Can you give the crusted sandwich to the dogs? (9)

4. Steve groaned because of the stains on his pants. (9)

More Challenging ☆ ☆

5. Sandy limped away clutching both of her crutches. (8)

6. Our teacher asked us to write both of the lists. (10)

7. Patrick fails because he does not study for the tests. (10)

8. Reading before you write helps you complete the essay faster. (10)

Most Challenging ★ ★ ☆

9 Buzz snitched that Jane was eating our treats before bedtime. (10)

10 Henry sketched the roses and will give a painting to his granny. (11)

11 The helper squinted at the list to see what he needed to make cupcakes. (14)

12 Kent has seen many beaches, but he likes staying at this one. (12)

Challenging Words ⭐

1st Syllable   2nd Syllable

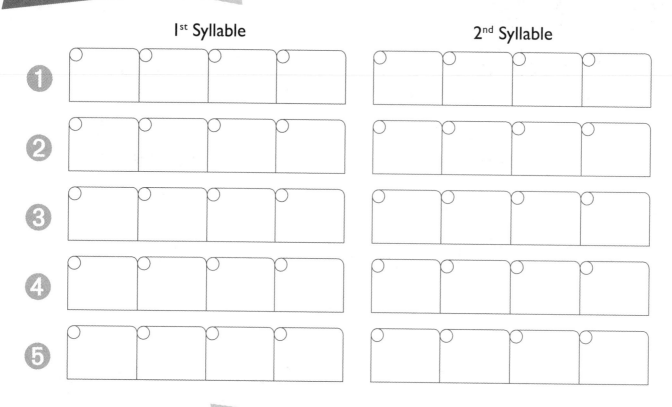

1
2
3
4
5

More Challenging Words ⭐⭐

1st Syllable   2nd Syllable

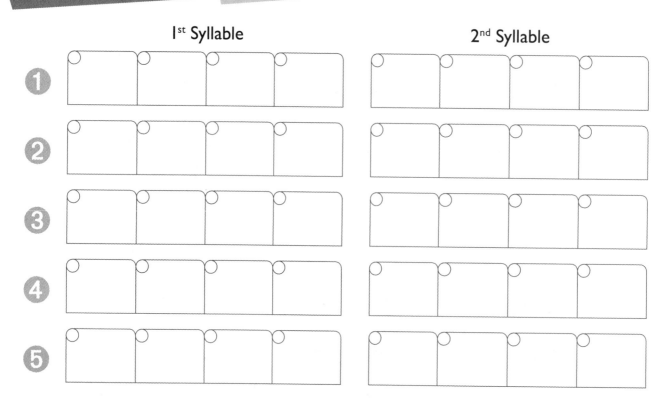

1
2
3
4
5

Mark It!

1. s o a k
2. s t i t c h
3. y e l l s
4. b r i d g e
5. s k a t e
6. f r i g h t
7. t w i s t
8. f r i z z
9. c r u n c h
10. r i s k s
11. c h e a t
12. b r a i d

Read It!

1. stitch   risks   twist
2. fright   soak   crunch
3. skate   risks   bridge
4. yells   twist   stitch
5. frizz   fright   cheat
6. soak   skate   yells
7. braid   crunch   frizz

Challenging

	1st Syllable				2nd Syllable				Schwa?
	Closed	Open	VCE	Vowel Team	Closed	Open	VCE	Vowel Team	
1 a•lone									
2 cup•cake									
3 dis•like									
4 ex•pand									

More Challenging ★★

	1st Syllable				2nd Syllable				Schwa?
	Closed	Open	VCE	Vowel Team	Closed	Open	VCE	Vowel Team	
1 pro•gram									
2 re•pay									
3 high•way									
4 lo•cate									

Most Challenging ★★★

	1st Syllable				2nd Syllable				Schwa?
	Closed	Open	VCE	Vowel Team	Closed	Open	VCE	Vowel Team	
1 a•fraid									
2 re•spond									
3 life•boat									
4 ath•lete									

Challenging ☆

1. hates to write essays

2. likes to eat frozen peaches

3. send the bugs down the drain

4. baby always fussed at midnight

More Challenging ☆ ☆

5. pays to stay in a clean motel

6. see the trapeze act in the parade

7. volume of the music was too high

8. sits in the backseat of the speedboat

Most Challenging ☆ ☆ ☆

9. salad with radish and beans for lunch

10. glass beads on her locket were broken

11. munching on pancakes and bacon for brunch

12. had a big fight while coaching the baseball team

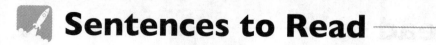

Challenging ☆

① Shine the light in the hole to locate it. (9)

② The baby only likes to eat frozen peaches. (8)

③ Brenda, is there a bean stuck in your throat? (9)

④ We like munching on pancakes and bacon for brunch. (9)

More Challenging ☆ ☆

⑤ Sammy, it is polite to invite Pete to the picnic. (10)

⑥ Dad yelled that the volume of the music was too high. (11)

⑦ The frozen soda fizzes and explodes when it defrosts. (9)

⑧ The delay of the plane will make us get to Tampa late. (12)

Most Challenging ☆ ☆ ☆

⑨ They like to buy jam and a loaf for toast at the roadside stand. (14)

⑩ Lee was happy that the glass beads on her locket were not broken. (13)

⑪ Was Steve high in the sky on the trapeze in the parade? (12)

⑫ Jean, was there a fight when you were coaching the baseball team? (12)

Challenging Words ☆

1.
2.
3.
4.
5.

More Challenging Words ☆ ☆

1st Syllable   2nd Syllable

1.
2.
3.
4.
5.

CELEBRATE!

Notes

Notes

My Heart Words

a · best · do · full · hot

about · better · does · funny · how

after · big · done · gave · hurt

again · black · don't · get · I

all · blue · down · give · if

always · both · draw · go · in

am · bring · drink · goes · into

an · brown · eat · going · is

and · but · eight · good · it

any · buy · every · got · its

are · by · fall · green · jump

around · call · far · grow · just

as · came · fast · had · keep

ask · can · find · has · kind

at · carry · first · have · know

ate · clean · five · he · laugh

away · cold · fly · help · let

be · come · for · her · light

because · could · found · here · like

been · cut · four · him · little

before · did · from · his · live

long